W9-BRJ-556

NATURE PROJECTS FOR EVERY SEASON

WINTER

by Phyllis S. Busch

illustrated by Megan Halsey

BENCHMARK BOOKS

MARSHALL CAVENDISH
NEW YORK

For my dear friend
Ruth Antine
— P. S. B.

To my sister
— M. H.

Benchmark Books
Marshall Cavendish Corporation
99 White Plains Road
Tarrytown, NY 10591

Printed in Hong Kong

Library of Congress Cataloging-in-Publication data
Busch, Phyllis S.
Winter / by Phyllis S. Busch ; illustrated by Megan Halsey.
p. cm. — (Nature projects for every season)
Includes bibliographical references and index.
Summary: Suggests a variety of outdoor and indoor activities for winter, focusing on science topics such as
animal behavior, the formation of icicles, frost pictures, and the nature of heat.
ISBN 0-7614-0989-0
1. Nature study—Activity programs—Juvenile literature. 2. Winter—Juvenile Literature.
[1. Winter. 2. Nature study] I. Halsey, Megan, ill. II. Title. III. Series.
QH81.B9937 1999 508.2—dc21 99-27466 CIP AC

CONTENTS

INTRODUCTION

Winter arrives on December 21. We have the shortest day and the longest night on that first day of winter. What causes these changes in the seasons?

The earth travels around the sun once a year. It slants, or tilts, as it travels. Winter comes when our part of the earth slants away from the sun. This gives us fewer hours of sunshine and the earth gets colder.

Many changes take place in winter. We wear woolen mittens, coats, hats, and boots. We get snow, ice, and frost. Some birds fly south. Other animals grow thicker coats. Some hide in burrows until it gets warmer again. There are no insects to be seen. Many trees are without leaves, and no wildflowers bloom.

We have a new and very different world to explore. There are many science and nature activities, both outdoors and indoors, to help us find out about this exciting winter season.

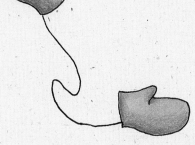

DECEMBER

				1	2	3	4
5	6	7	8	9	10	11	
12	13	14	15	16	17	18	
19	20	21	22	23	24	25	
26	27	28	29	30	31		

5

OUTDOOR ACTIVITIES

SIGNS OF WILDLIFE IN WINTER

Winter is a quiet season outdoors. Most wild animals are not very active. Some animals have gone south for the winter. Some hibernate in their dens until spring. Others have built warm winter homes where they can be protected from the cold and snow. They leave their homes when they have to feed. Rabbits, squirrels, deer, and certain birds are some of the animals who remain active all winter.

We can hunt for clues left by these and other wildlife. How many signs of wildlife can you find? Plan to explore a number of different areas. Examine such places as gardens, trees, fields, birdfeeding stations, woods, roadways, ponds, streams, parking lots, and the area around your house. You will need a pad, a pencil, and a copy of the SIGNS OF WILDLIFE on the next page.

You will probably wish to go on several such hunting trips throughout the season. Keep a record of the date for each discovery.

deer droppings

hornet's nest

crow tracks

rabbit droppings

SIGNS OF WILDLIFE

A SQUIRREL'S WINTER HOME (Look for a large round bunch of leaves and twigs high up in a tree.)

OLD BIRD NESTS (Nests are found in trees, bushes, on windowsills.)

HOLES IN TREES (Made by woodpeckers. Some are large and some small.)

A HORNET'S NEST (Hornets are dead by the middle of winter.)

TORN WEBS ON TREE BRANCHES (Leftover webs from the fall webworm, an insect.)

A BIRD'S FEATHER ON THE GROUND

DEER DROPPINGS (These resemble chocolate-covered peanuts.)

RABBIT DROPPINGS (These look like chocolate-covered M & M's.)

COCOONS ON TWIGS (Look for little cases attached to twigs on bushes, on trees, or lying on the ground.)

ROUND BALLS ON THE STEM OF A GOLDENROD (A little fly spends the winter in these dwellings.)

A BAND OF SHINY BLACK EGGS AROUND A TWIG (These are the tiny eggs of the tent caterpillar.)

A MASS OF TAN-COLORED EGGS ON A TREE TRUNK (Eggs of the gypsy moth.)

TWIGS TORN BY DEER (Edges are jagged, made by the deer's back teeth.)

TWIGS CUT BY RABBITS (Edges are sharp and slanting, made by the rabbit's front teeth.)

TRACKS IN THE SNOW MADE BY BIRDS (Look for sets of two legs. Also look for marks of the wings of birds.)

TRACKS IN THE SNOW LEFT BY RABBITS, DEER, MICE, OTHERS (Look for sets of four legs.)

LIST ADDITIONAL SIGNS OF WILDLIFE THAT YOU HAVE DISCOVERED

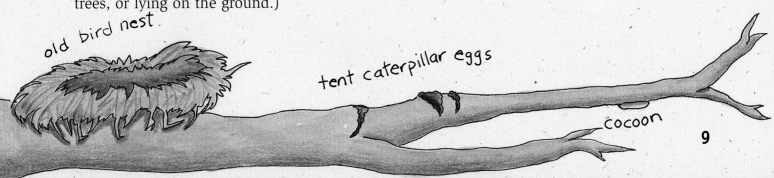

old bird nest

tent caterpillar eggs

cocoon

HOW COLD IS IT OUTDOORS?

It is winter and your outdoor thermometer shows that it is cold. It reads a little above 32°F (or a little above 0°C). Many thermometers have both scales. Is the outdoor temperature the same everywhere?

You can find out by checking the temperature outdoors in many different places. You will need a thermometer, a pad, and a pencil. Pick a cold sunny day above freezing weather. Dress warmly and visit a number of places to take a temperature reading. Record the date, location, and the temperature. Make a record of both scales if your thermometer has both.

Here are some places to check: in your hallway, on the outside of your house where the sun is shining, on the side in the shade, above a paved road, above a dirt road, above a lawn, among a group of trees, in a bush, above the edge of a pond, in an empty bird nest, inside a parked car in the sun and one in the shade, inside your glove or mitten on your hand and off your hand, in a pocket of your jacket. You can probably think of many other different places.

Where is it the coldest? Which is the warmest spot? Where did you feel most comfortable? Can you explain why the temperatures were different in the various places?

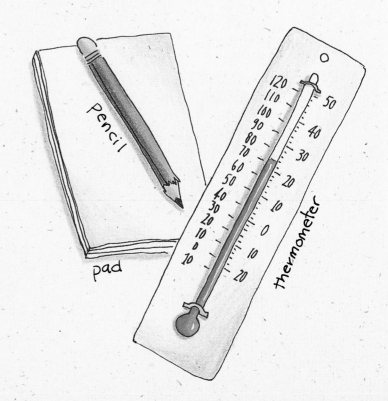

SNOW FLEAS

Snow fleas are tiny wingless insects that live underground. They feed on decaying leaves and rotten wood. During the winter, however, they may suddenly appear on top of the snow. Look for these small six-legged creatures on one of your walks this winter.

The best time to find snow fleas is during a winter thaw. The ground remains covered with snow, but the temperature is a little above freezing. Snow begins to melt.

This is when millions of snow fleas come up through cracks in the snow. They march on top of the snow in masses. It looks as if the white snow has turned black where the insects move. Perhaps they are searching for food. No one is sure why these marches take place.

Take a close look at some snow fleas. Notice that they jump. The insects have an active tail that they use to spring forward. Another name for them is springtails.

You can roll some up in a snowball, take the ball home and put it in a freezer overnight. Place the snowball in a dish the next day where you can examine the snowfleas more closely with a magnifying glass. Its tail remains folded under its body when it is not being used.

magnified snow flea

LET'S LOOK AT SNOWFLAKES

You know it is snowing when you see the snowflakes falling. They fall very quietly. You can hear it raining but you cannot hear it snowing. Snowflakes are beautiful. Go out to examine some snowflakes during a snowfall. Make sure to dress warmly.

You will need a black piece of paper on which to catch snowflakes. You can also catch snowflakes on dark gloves or coat sleeves.

Catch some snowflakes on your paper, gloves, or coat sleeve and look at them close-up. Snowflakes are made of ice. See how the ice makes them shine in the sunlight.

The snowflakes look like dainty pieces of lace. Each snowflake has six sides but the design of each one is different. How many different kinds of snowflakes can you find?

Try to examine the snowflakes at the beginning of a snowstorm and at the end of the storm. What differences do you see in the snowflakes?

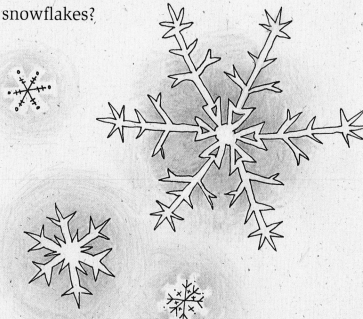

12

WHERE DO ICICLES FORM?

Icicles sparkle in the sun and make the winter landscape more beautiful. Icicles form when snow melts and begins to turn into water. The water drips downward. First one drop freezes, then another, and another, and the icicle grows longer. There are very small icicles as well as huge ones.

There are many interesting things to observe about icicles. Go out on a day when there is plenty of snow. The weather should be freezing but sunny. Take a walk to find out some interesting things about icicles.

Where do icicles form? Look on the edges of roofs, on bare tree branches, and on the bumpers of cars.

Where did you find the longest icicle? the shortest?

Find a roof where the snow is melting even though it is cold enough for water to freeze. Why did it melt? It could be the sun on the outside or the heat on the inside. In some places it may be both.

Look for icicles that are bent into different shapes. When did the bending take place, before or after the icicle formed? Try to bend an icicle. What happens? How might the wind have caused the icicle to bend?

MAKE AN ICICLE

You can make an icicle if the weather is below freezing. You will need an open clean can, a piece of string to make a handle by which to hang the can, a hammer, a large nail and cold water.

Ask an adult to make a hole in the center of the bottom and two holes near the top of the can. The holes can be made by hammering the nail through the can. Pull the piece of string through the two top holes. Fill the can with cold water. You can also use an old toy pail instead of a can.

Find a place to hang the can or pail of water so that you can see it from inside your house. The water will begin to drip from the bottom hole and freeze to form an icicle. If it is a windy day the icicle may bend as it freezes.

Try to make a rainbow of icicles. Rainbows have seven colors: violet, indigo, blue, green, orange, yellow, red. Make as many of the rainbow-colored icicles as you can. Prepare a can of water as described above for each color. Color the water with paint or food coloring. Hang the cans in a row on a clothesline. It will be interesting to see a row of rainbow-colored icicles.

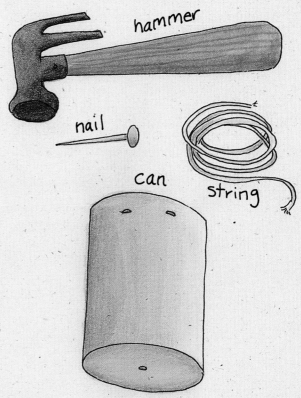

hammer

nail

string

can

17

BOOT PRINTS IN THE SNOW

The world outdoors looks different after a snowfall. Snow covers all surfaces and fills all the cracks. The broken fence and the abandoned car are covered. The heap of rubbish and the untidy street look clean and fresh.

Whatever moves over the snow leaves its mark. It may be a truck, skis, or people's shoes.

The bottoms of snow boots have many different designs. It is fun to learn to recognize the marks left by someone's boot print.

Plan to meet a group of friends outside after a freshly fallen snow. Everyone should be wearing snow boots. Examine the marks in the snow left by your own boot print. Then everyone look at each other's.

Form a circle. One at a time, each member of the group walks a few steps on a new patch of snow. Then everyone examines that boot print. After all have their turn, walk across a fresh snow-covered area. Try to identify the boot wearers by the tracks left by their boots.

ANIMAL TRACKS IN THE SNOW

Explore the snow tracks left by animals. You can recognize the footprints left by birds. Birds usually have four toes, three in front and one behind. Some birds walk and some birds hop.

The walkers place one foot ahead of the other, leaving a single row of tracks. Pigeons, crows, and starlings are walkers. Hoppers leave paired tracks because they land with both feet on the snow. Sparrows and juncos are hoppers.

You will also find the tracks of four-legged animals. The tracks that you see most often are those of cats, dogs, mice, squirrels, and rabbits. They all leave set of four tracks, each with a different pattern.

The long hind legs of a rabbit leave two long tracks followed by two small round ones made by the front legs. Look at the direction of the rabbit's round tracks to find out which way it was traveling.

Mice and squirrels make tracks in paired sets of four.

Cats and dogs walk on their toes. Dogs leave tracks that show their claw marks. Cats walk in a single file, pulling their claws in, so their tracks show no claw marks.

After you learn to recognize some tracks, your snow walks will become more exciting as you try to figure out the stories left by tracks in the snow. And there are always new tracks to be discovered.

squirrel tracks

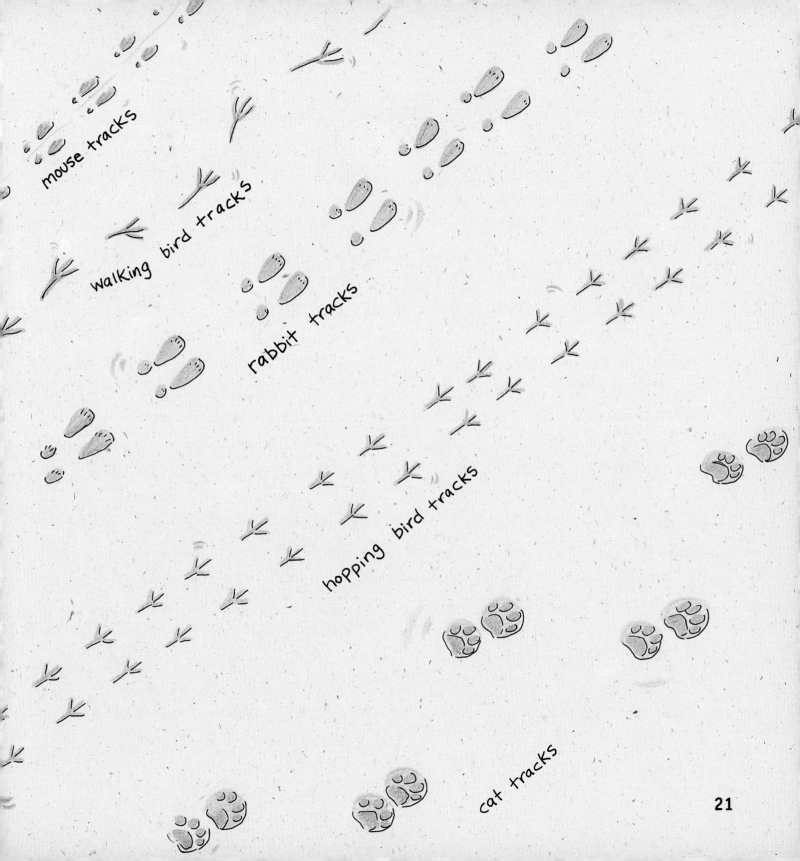

mouse tracks

walking bird tracks

rabbit tracks

hopping bird tracks

cat tracks

21

EXAMINE SOME LEAVES ON THE SNOW

Leaves that are found on top of the snow do not remain on top. They are found in depressions, or hollows, in the snow. Some leaves lie deeper than others. Leaves are very light. They are not heavy enough to press the snow down. They sink because of the sun's heat. Even though it is freezing outside, the sun's energy reaches the earth.

Plan to find out more about this by carrying out a simple investigation. You will need about six metal disks such as the tops of fruit juice cans. Have an adult help you to paint each disk with a different color. Be sure to paint one black and another one white. The others can be any colors you choose. Plan to go outdoors on a very sunny winter day when there is snow on the ground.

Find a level sunny spot that has some leaves on top of the snow. Arrange the disks in a row on the snow with a little space between each. They should remain there for about fifteen minutes. You can examine the leaves on the snow while you wait.

How far down below the surface are the leaves? You will find that the darker leaves lie deeper than the lighter ones. All the leaves absorb heat from the sunshine. Darker leaves absorb more heat than lighter ones. The heat melts the snow beneath them and the leaves sink.

Return to examine the painted disks on the snow. Which one sank the most? Which one sank the least? How far down are the others?

Now you can understand why dark coats are warmer than light ones. You probably have noticed that black cars heat up faster than white cars. All this heat comes from the sun all year.

TINY BIRD SHAPES ON THE SNOW

Birch trees shed their seeds in winter. Birch seeds form in small, dark, slender hanging bundles called catkins. They are about as large as the pinkie of your hand. The catkin is made up of very small seeds that are protected by scales. These scales have the shape of little birds. They are called mimic birds.

Take a walk to search for mimic birds. You may want to take a magnifying glass with you in order to see them more clearly. Find a birch tree. White birches are easier to spot than black birches but both have catkins.

Look on the snow beneath the tree. Does it look as if someone sprinkled pepper on the snow? These are the mimic birds. Look carefully to find the seeds, which are smaller, paler, and round.

Try to reach a catkin hanging on the tree. Remove it and break it apart to examine how the seeds and the scales are arranged. Crush the catkin and scatter the seeds and mimic birds on the snow.

The seeds will sink into the earth when the snow melts. Each seed can grow into a new birch tree if it has enough room, water, and sunshine.

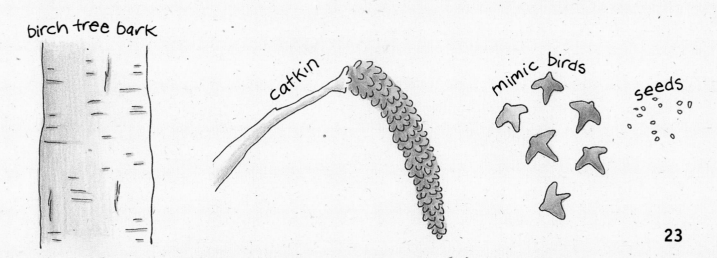

birch tree bark

catkin

mimic birds

seeds

CHRISTMAS TREES

The brightly colored leaves of fall are gone. The trees from which they fell remain bare all winter. Evergreen trees are green all year. They stand out very clearly now. These are the trees we use as Christmas trees. Evergreens do lose their leaves but not all at once. You will find old fallen leaves under the trees.

The leaves of evergreen trees are very narrow. They have a coat of wax that protects them from the cold. Pine trees are evergreens that have round narrow leaves called needles. They grow in little bundles. Other evergreen trees have small flat leaves that grow singly, not in bundles. The evergreens bear their seeds in cones.

Get acquainted with some evergreen trees in your neighborhood. Look at the needles of pine trees. How many are there in a bundle? Compare them with the small flat leaves of the evergreens. Collect some cones from each tree. You will find them on the ground among the fallen needles. Carry some home where it will be warmer and you can examine them more closely. Compare the cones and the leaves with the picture shown here.

Take along a copy of the pictures and a bag for collecting cones.

WHITE PINE—Five needles to a bundle. Cones are long and narrow.

PITCH PINE—Three needles in a bundle. Cones are prickly.

SPRUCE—Leaves are stiff, sharp, and do not grow in a bundle. Cones may be small or long (as in Norway spruce).

HEMLOCK—Short flat leaves grow singly. Cones are very small.

white pine

pitch pine

spruce

hemlock

AN UNUSUAL TREASURE HUNT

This is a treasure hunt where you find your very own treasure. Plan to go hunting with a group of friends. They will all search for a personal treasure. Choose a familiar place, one that you all know very well. Walk slowly and quietly. Examine everything as if you were in a strange land for the first time. Look overhead and underfoot as well as straight ahead. You are searching for something special that you will remember the rest of your life.

Here are some suggestions: a special stone, the way the sun strikes the trunk of a tree, the shape of a cloud, a bird flying above you, the look and sound of a running brook, the shape of a bare tree, the collection of plants on a large rock. There are many things to catch your eye. Just look. When you have found your treasure, stand still and look or think about it for a few minutes.

The whole group should get together after everyone is finished. Each person tells about his or her find. You can visit each other's treasure if there is time and you are not too cold.

Whenever you feel unhappy about something, think about your treasure. It may cheer you up.

INDOOR ACTIVITIES

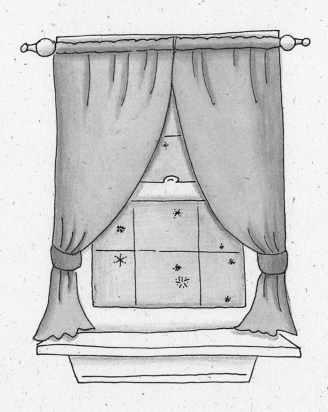

PREPARE A WINTER TREAT FOR THE BIRDS

Birds need winter food that will provide them with warmth and energy. Suet is the best source for this. They also need something to grind and help them digest their food, such as sand. This can be either beach sand or box sand. Prepare a special treat to attract birds that remain here all winter. This is a project for you to do with the help of adults.

You will need one and a half cups raw suet, two cups bread crumbs, one cup popped corn, one cup sunflower seeds, and one teaspoon sand. You will also need a netted suet bag or the netting that onions and grapes sometimes come in, in which to put the food when it is done, a piece of wax paper, a fork, and a double boiler.

Mix the bread crumbs, popcorn, and sunflower seeds in a bowl. Have an adult help you to cut it into tiny pieces and melt it in the top of a double boiler. Remove it from the stove. Let it harden a little. Then reheat it and pour it over the dry ingredients in the bowl. Sprinkle the sand over it and mix it with a fork. Turn it out on the wax paper and press it to form a ball.

Put the ball in the refrigerator until it is firm. Put it in the netted bag and then hang it out for the birds to enjoy.

suet

breadcrumbs

popcorn

sunflowers seeds

sand

net bag

double boiler

fork

Waxpaper

HOW SAFE IS IT TO EAT SNOW?

March is when maple syrup is made from the sap of maple trees. In colonial days children enjoyed a special treat at this time. Thick hot maple syrup was poured over clean snow to be enjoyed as a kind of sundae. Would that be safe for you to eat today?

To find out you need two clean jars, two paper towels, two rubber bands, and some clean snow.

Cover the openings of the jars with the paper towels. Drape the towels loosely, leaving a depression, or dent, on top. Keep them in place with the rubber bands. Place the same amount of snow on each paper towel. Examine the towels after all the snow melts. You will find a collection of dirt in place of the snow. This should convince you that snow is not good to eat.

You may want to repeat this investigation with snow from different places. You will find that snow in some areas has more dirt than in other places. How does snow get dirty?

jars

rubber
bands

paper
towels

snow

30

HOW MUCH WATER IS THERE IN SNOW?

Snow turns to water when it melts. How much water is there in snow? To find out you will need a quart jar, water, a cup, and some snow.

First fill the jar with water. How many cups of water does the jar hold? You will measure four cups of water. Now pack the empty jar with snow. Put the jar in a warm place until all the snow has melted. Pour the water into the cup. This will give you an idea of how much water there is in snow.

Try the same thing with fresh snow and with old snow. Which has more water? How much water do you get from a cup of snow?

snow melting in a jar

MAKE SOME PAPER SNOWFLAKES

Snowflakes come in a variety of shapes and with many different designs. The flakes grow as they fall through the air. Each snowflake has six sides no matter what form it takes.

Here are some snowflake designs, each showing six identical sides.

You can make some pretty snowflakes of your own out of paper. All you need is some paper, a plate, a pencil, and a pair of scissors. Your snowflake will be the same size as the plate.

Place the plate upside down on the paper and draw a circle around it. Cut out the circle. Fold the circle exactly in half. Then fold it again in three equal parts. It will resemble the shape of an ice-cream cone.

Cut different shapes to make a design. Unfold the paper to admire your snowflake.

You may wish to try plates of various sizes and use different kinds of paper.

paper circle

folded in half

folded in three equal parts

WHAT HAPPENS TO WATER WHEN IT FREEZES?

Two interesting things happen to water when it freezes. Find out what they are. You will need a paper cup, a glass jar with a cover, a crayon, and water.

Fill the cup with water up to the top. Pour water only halfway into the jar and cover the jar. Draw a line on the side of the jar with your crayon [pencil] to mark the top of the water. Place both the cup and the jar in the freezer overnight. Remove them the next day.

You will find the water in the cup has turned to ice and the ice has risen above the top of the cup. The water in the jar has also turned into a solid block of ice and is taking up more room in the jar. How much above the water level mark has it risen?

Now you know two things that happen to water when it freezes. It turns to ice and it takes up more room because it gets larger. Water expands when it freezes. This is the reason why water pipes burst when the water in them freezes.

Try this to see the power of water when it freezes. Get a small plastic jar with a screw top. Fill it with water. Screw the top on tightly. Put it in the freezer overnight.

What happened? The sides of the container were pushed out by the expanding ice inside. Perhaps the plastic sides split open.

Water that gets into cracks in rocks outdoors can freeze in winter and split the rocks apart. This can happen to bricks, driveways, and paved walks.

water paper cup crayon jar with cover

TRY THIS TRICK WITH AN ICE CUBE

Add an ice cube to a glass of water. Ice is frozen water. The ice cube floats because water become lighter when it freezes. The trick is to remove the ice cube from the glass of water using only a string and a pinch of salt. The string should be about six inches (fifteen centimeters) long.

Wet the center of the string. Lay it across the top of an ice cube with the wet part of the string touching the ice cube. The rest of the string will dangle down the sides of the glass. Sprinkle a pinch of salt over the ice cube. Wait a few seconds. The ice under the salt melts and refreezes around the string. Now you can lift the ice cube with the string.

Try this another way. Moisten the end of the string and lift the ice cube as it dangles from the end. This looks more impressive.

In many places road crews spread salt on snow-covered roads because salt melts the snow. However, the salt harms the trees and other plants growing along the roads. It would be better to use safer methods of snow removal. Some communities use ashes.

FIND LIFE UNDER THE SNOW

Snow covers soil, dead leaves, and rotting wood. Under the snow is a winter hiding place for many small animals. You can find insects, spiders, centipedes, and others. Examine some of these organisms with a magnifying glass.

You will need a waterproof bag, a shovel, a shallow pan, plastic wrap, a pencil and paper, and a magnifying glass.

Go out with your shovel and collecting bag. Dig up some dead leaves and plants below the snow. Put it into your bag to take home. Empty the bag into the pan and cover the pan with the plastic until everything has defrosted.

You will find many kinds of small animals. Examine them with a magnifying glass. You can identify an insect if the animal has six legs. A spider has eight legs and a centipede has many more legs.

Make a record of the date, the place from which the material was dug, and what you found. Draw some sketches of the animals.

You may wish to examine more samples of frozen material beneath the snow. Look at some that comes from sunny areas or from the shade. Find out if there are different creatures below the snow along a stream or a pond.

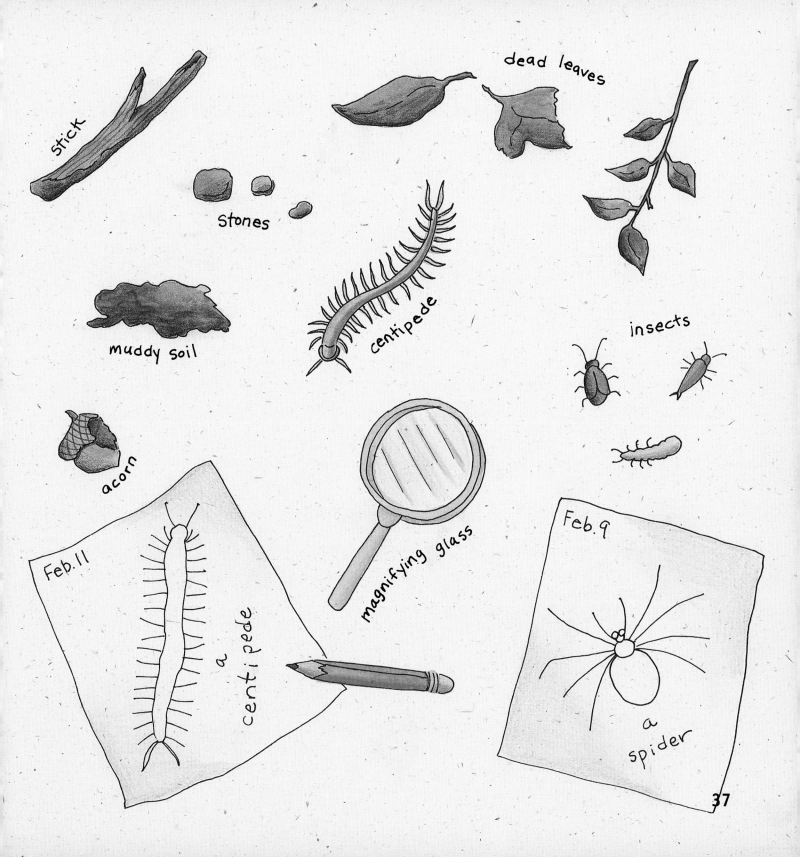

stick

dead leaves

stones

muddy soil

centipede

insects

acorn

magnifying glass

Feb. 11

a centipede

Feb. 9

a spider

37

MAKE FROST PICTURES ON A WINDOWPANE

Perhaps you have noticed pretty frost pictures on some windows in your house when it is very cold. The pictures look like lace or delicate ferns and stars. This often happens in the middle of winter. The etchings usually form at night. It is best to see them very early in the morning before they melt.

Get close to the window and blow warm breath from your mouth on the picture. This should melt the frost. Another way to do this is to ask an adult to hold a hair dryer close enough to the glass for the frost to melt.

Step away from the window as soon as the picture or part of it is gone. Another will immediately appear in the bare spot to take its place. New shapes will form around the melted place. You will probably discover all kinds of new designs.

Frost pictures form when it is freezing outdoors and the windows are cold and moist on the inside.

HOW DO YOU KEEP THINGS FROM LOSING HEAT?

You may wish to keep your lunch from getting too cold. You can put it into an insulated bag. Or you may wish to keep your body warm on a cold winter day. You could wear a woolen or fleece coat and hat. These materials prevent the loss of heat. We call them insulation materials.

What provides good insulation? Here is an interesting way to find out. You will need four small jars or plastic vials, all the same size, four rubber bands, and snow. You will also need pieces of the following insulating materials, each large enough to wrap around a container: wool, paper, aluminum foil, cotton.

Pack the containers full of snow. Wrap each in a different piece of the insulating materials. Put them in a warm place for a while. Unwrap them to see how much water is in each one. Which has the least amount of water? Which has the greatest amount of water? The container with the most water was wrapped in the poorest insulation material. It allowed the snow to melt most rapidly.

You may wish to test other materials that you have in your home to find out whether any are good for insulation.

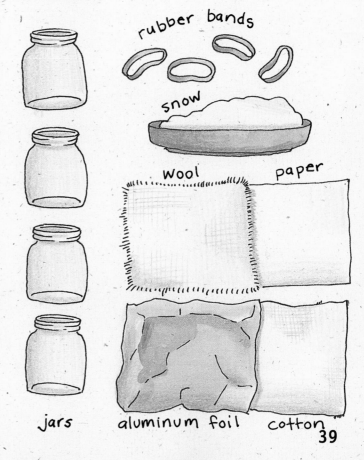

HOW WARM IS YOUR HOUSE?

You will need paper, a pencil, and a thermometer. There are Fahrenheit and Celsius thermometers. Many thermometers are made with both scales. Find out what kind of thermometer you will be using.

Place a thermometer on a wall in one of your rooms at home. Hang it so that it is level with your eyes. This will make it easy to see. Leave the thermometer in place for a few minutes before reading the temperature. Write the name of the room and the temperature for that room. Do the same for several rooms. You will probably find that each room has a different temperature. Which room is the warmest? Which is the coldest?

Now select one of the rooms and take the air temperature in several places in that one room. Make a list of the places you plan to check and write the temperature of each one.

Here are some suggestions: What is the temperature at eye level at each of the four walls? Down near the floor? Near the door? Near each window? Near a source of heat? Near the ceiling? (Do this with the help of an adult.) Think of other locations in the room where you can read the air temperature and add them to your list of places.

Look at your list. How do you explain the different temperatures in different parts of the room?

HOW CAN YOU STOP DRAFTS IN A ROOM?

Some rooms are uncomfortable in winter because they are drafty. You feel chilled by small currents of cold air. These may be blowing from under a door or from a windowsill. One way to stop such drafts is to make a draft stopper.

You will need a narrow tube that is as long as the windowsill or the bottom of the door. The tube should be wide enough for your hand to squeeze through the opening. You will also need a needle, thread, scissors, and some insulating material such as sawdust, dry sand, pieces of roof insulation, pillow stuffing, or bubble plastic that is used for packaging.

The tube can be made from any sturdy fabric or you can try to use an old stocking. Ask an adult to help you sew the tube tightly if you are making it from fabric. Stuff the tube tightly with insulation material.

Finish the draft stopper by sewing the opening.

Place the draft stopper snugly against the drafty crack. Maybe your draft stopper will make the room more comfortable.

DRAW A PICTURE OF A SNOW SCENE

It is winter. The ground is covered with snow and the sun is shining brightly. This is a good time to draw a picture of a snow scene as you see it through one of your windows.

Select some white and colored sheets of drawing paper, a set of colored crayons, a pencil, and a board on which you can place your paper. Look through each window in your house until you find a scene that you would like to draw. Make a sketch of the scene with your pencil, then add whatever colors you need to finish it.

Draw the same view on papers of different colors. Shadows change as the sun moves daily across the sky. Make some drawings of the same scene at different times of day to show the changing shadows. Perhaps you would like to paint the same view with watercolors.

These are a few ways in which to keep a record of a pretty scene. Can you think of others?

white paper

colored papers

crayons

pencil

board

START TO KEEP A SCIENCE AND NATURE DIARY

A science and nature diary is a written record of what you do in science and nature, both outdoors and indoors. You will need a notebook or a pad that you will use only for writing your diary.

You may write in your diary every day or every few days. Always write the date first. Then tell what you did or saw or heard that day. You may also wish to describe how you feel about your experience. Illustrate your writing with a drawing or a poem, if you wish. Here is a sample page from a science and nature diary.

Wednesday, December 3, 1997

It was very cold and freezing today. The ground was covered with snow. I took a short walk with my father to look for icicles. We found many of them. Some hung down from the edges of roofs. I also saw some hanging from the ledges of windows. I asked my father if he would help me make some icicles when we returned home. He said that he would.

We went home to find an open can. My father made two holes near the top of the can with an ice pick. Then he fastened the ends of a piece of wire to the holes to make a handle. He also made a hole in the bottom of the can and I filled the can with water.

We found a hook outside on which my father hung the can of water. Then we went inside where we could look at the can through the window. It was too cold to stay outside. My father said that it was below freezing. The water began to drip and freeze into an icicle.

SOME READING SUGGESTIONS

Asch, Frank. *Sawgrass Poems*. New York: Harcourt Brace and Co., 1996.

Busch, Phyllis S. *Backyard Safaris*. New York: Simon and Schuster, 1995.

Casey, Denise. *Weather Everywhere*. New York: Macmillian, 1995.

Docekal, Eileen M. *Nature Detective*. New York: Sterling Pub. Co., 1989.

Gibbons, Gail. *The Reasons for Seasons*. New York: Holiday House, 1995.

Lauber, Patricia. *Earthworms*. Woodbridge, Conn.: Blackbirch Press, 1994.

Pascoe, Elaine. *Butterflies and Moths*. Woodbridge, Conn.: Blackbirch Press, 1996.

———. *Tadpoles*. Woodbridge, Conn.: Blackbirch Press, 1996.

———. *Seeds and Seedlings*. Woodbridge, Conn.: Blackbirch Press, 1997.

Willis, Nancy Carol. *The Robins in Your Backyard*. Montchanin, Del.: Cucumber Island Storytellers, 1996.

INDEX

Page numbers for illustrations are in boldface